Contents

Hey little human,
do you want to make noises
like the wild animals of the world?
Get ready to hoot
and purr and squeak.
Get ready to whoop and roar...
let's hear!

SING
LIKE A
WHALE

Moira Butterfield

Illustrated by Gwen Millward

WELBECK
EDITIONS

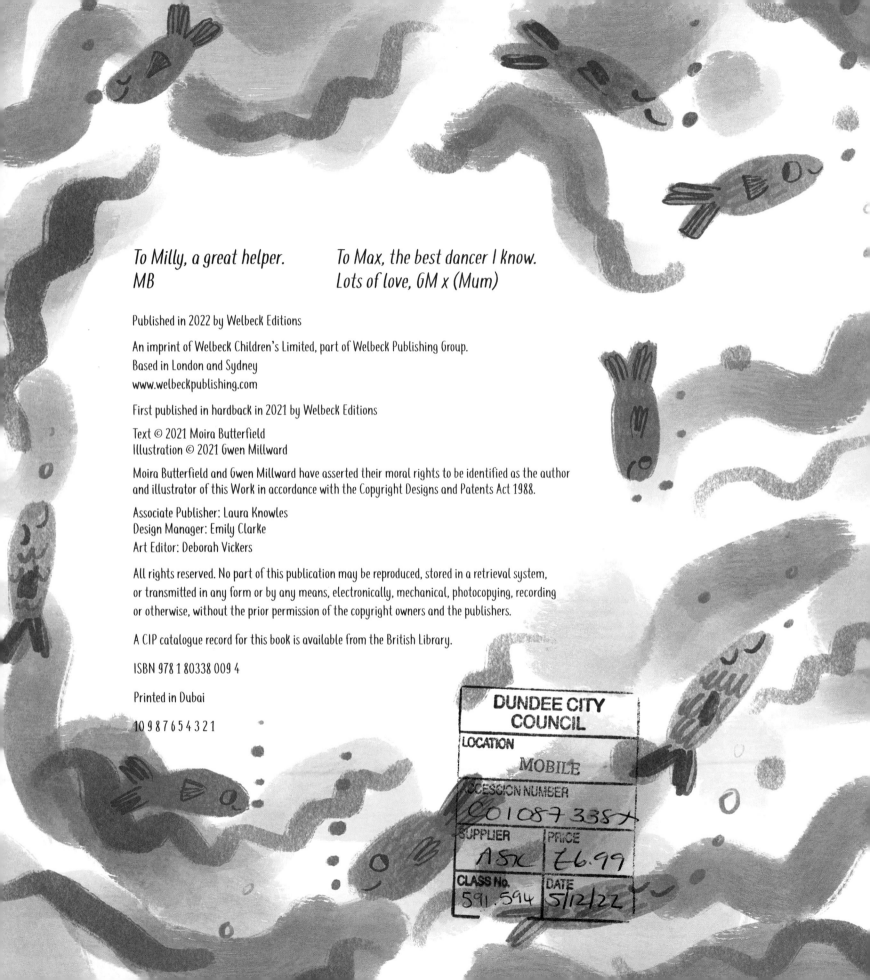

To Milly, a great helper.
MB

To Max, the best dancer I know.
Lots of love, GM x (Mum)

Published in 2022 by Welbeck Editions

An imprint of Welbeck Children's Limited, part of Welbeck Publishing Group.
Based in London and Sydney
www.welbeckpublishing.com

First published in hardback in 2021 by Welbeck Editions

Text © 2021 Moira Butterfield
Illustration © 2021 Gwen Millward

Moira Butterfield and Gwen Millward have asserted their moral rights to be identified as the author
and illustrator of this Work in accordance with the Copyright Designs and Patents Act 1988.

Associate Publisher: Laura Knowles
Design Manager: Emily Clarke
Art Editor: Deborah Vickers

A CIP catalogue record for this book is available from the British Library.

ISBN 978 1 80338 009 4

Printed in Dubai

10 9 8 7 6 5 4 3 2 1

A **humpback whale** (a male whale)
might want to call his humpback friends.
But how, when the sea's so wide?
Easy! He sings through the water.
Hooooooooo. Hooooooooo. Long and low.
Can you do the same?
Let's hear!

Swim around like a whale with flappy flippers.

Call for a friend. Hoooo! Hoooo!

Hoooooo

Hooooo

Look out for another whale...

Sing a hello! Hoooo! Hoooo!

Lions live in families.
The biggest one is father lion.
He likes to shake his shaggy mane
and tell us all how strong he is.
Roar! Roar! I'm the loudest!
Can you do the same?
Let's hear!

Lie down like a sleeping lion.

Wake up and shake your mane.

Stand up and look proud.
Get ready...

Roar!
Roar!

An **owl** will have a special home —
a tall spreading tree, maybe.
It won't share with other owls.
It tells them all to stay away.
Hoot, hoot! My tree! **Mine!**
Can you do the same?
Let's hear!

Put your arms down by your sides
to look like a perching owl.
Turn your head this way and that.

Signal to the other owls.
Hoot, hoot! Hoot, hoot!

Hoot,
Hoot!

Now stretch your wings
and glide away!

Wolves live in furry packs.
They get together, under the moon,
to howl – like singing with their friends.
A-woooooooo!
A-wooooooooo!
They all join in.
Can you do the same?
Let's hear!

Creep, creep... like a wolf
hunting in the forest.

Look up at the silvery moon.

Now sit, little wolf!

A-woo!
A-woo!

It's howling time. A-wooo! A-wooo!

It's early morning. The sun is rising.
What's that noise? A **kookaburra** call!
It's like a laugh... *Ah, ah, ah!*
It really means:
Don't come near!
Can you do the same?
Let's hear!

Hop around your favourite spot
like a busy, bossy bird.

Dip your head to peck for food.
You like spiders, ants and worms!

Stop to listen for other birds.
You're grumpy about them
coming close.

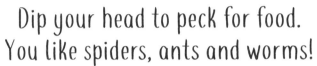

Call out in case they are near.
Ah, ah, ah! I rule here!

When a **chick** is going to hatch
it peck, peck, pecks inside its egg.
Crack! The crunchy shell breaks up
and the tiny chick hops out.
Peep, peep, peep! It calls for Mum.
Can you do the same?
Let's hear!

Pretend to crack your egg. Peck, peck.

Hatch out and stretch your wings.

Peep,
  peep,
    peep!

Call for Mum. Peep, peep, peep!

Peep,
  peep,
    peep!

Shake your tail feathers.
Peep, peep, peep!

Here comes a **gibbon**, swinging smoothly
between the branches. What long arms!
It's calling loudly. What's it saying?
Whoop, whoop!
I found some fruit.
Can you do the same?
Let's hear!

Hold your arms high, like a gibbon.

Pretend you're swinging through
the trees.

Point to a tree that's full of fruit.

Whoop,   whoop!

Now tell your friends.
Whoop, whoop!

Next time you meet a friendly **cat**
stroke it just behind its ears.
If it starts to purr...
Prrrrrrrr...
It's saying *Aah! That makes me happy.*
Can you do the same?
Let's hear!

Tiptoe, tiptoe silently,
as if you are a creeping cat.

Rub your cheek with your paw
to smooth down your fluffy fur.

Find a soft, comfy place
to curl up on your side.

Prrrrrrr, prrrrrrr!

Purr to show you're feeling fine.
Prrrrrrr, prrrrrrr! Happy cat!

Horses like to be with friends,
munching grass or playing chase,
having fun in their field.
When they meet, they say hello
with a **whinny** – high then low.
Can you do the same?
Let's hear!

Trot around your grassy field.
Clip, clop. Clip, clop.

Kick out your leg and
shake your mane.

whinny   whinny

Here comes another horse.
Whinny! Whinny! Say hello.

Gallop-a-gallop-a-gallop-a-gallop.
Race your friend across your field.

A **snake** is sleeping in the sun
when she's woken by a sound.
She makes a hissing warning noise.
Hissssss. Hisssssss. Keep away!
I'll bite if I get a fright.
Can you do the same?
Let's hear!

Curl up like a sleepy snake.

Wake up! Wake up!
Something's coming!

Stretch your head up high
and hissssss!

Hisssssss!

Quick! Slither and slide away!

Trit-trot. Trit-trot.

Here's a **goat** with a hairy beard.
He's hungry, so he starts to bleat.
Meh, meh! Meh, meh!
Where's all the juicy grass?
Can you do the same?
Let's hear!

Trit-trot like a goat, with your
fingers up like horns.

Dip your head to show your horns.
What a fine goat you are!

Meh, Meh!

Meh, Meh!

Tell everyone you're feeling hungry.
Meh, meh! Meh, meh!

Now nibble on some juicy grass.
Nom, nom. Nom, nom!

Mice like to hurry and scurry,
looking for food and spots to nest.
A furry family of mice
will squeak to each other as they explore.
Squeak, squeak! *Follow me!*
Can you do the same?
Let's hear!

Hold up your arms, tight to your chest.
Be a mouse, looking for a house.

Scurry around, this way and that.

Squeak,

squeak!

Squeak, squeak!

Signal to your family.
Squeak, squeak! Squeak, squeak!

Squeak, squeak!

Settle in a sleeping spot.
Squeak, squeak! Goodnight, mouse!

Hey, **little human**, the world is wide.
There are lots more creatures for you to meet
and lots more noises for you to make.
But...

Now it's time to make your sound.
Sing a song. Sing to say:
I'm feeling really good today!
Are you ready?
Let's hear!

"Naa, Naa! Nee, nee!
I'm a human. Sing with me!"

Peep,

peep,

peep!